Introduction

Ever since I was a small kid I have been interested in police work. Every family event my grandfather and my uncle would discuss some stories about their daily lives and what they saw during the day as police officers. I have always admired the dedication it takes to do the job and I have met multiple police officers throughout my childhood and every single one of them are the nicest men and women I have met.

Part of my project was getting some experience in the police field of work. My mentor was K9 officer Brandon Cox and he was an absolute fantastic mentor. He was super friendly and I got to see a solid day of work that he did everyday. To start the day, we helped this man that had a heart attack while driving. He had pulled to the side of the road and another man who was driving behind him noticed the man was in trouble. He called 911 and tried to help the man until we arrived. Officer Cox performed CPR until the ambulance got there. The man ended up surviving, which we found out later that day. Throughout the rest of the day, we went through multiple traffic stops and I saw how common procedures took place. One of the best things of the entire ride-along was riding with Officer Cox's K9, Aries. Aries was such a good dog and super fun to be around. While he did bark a lot, it was cool to see the bond Officer Cox had with Aries. He was friendly to me as well once he got used to me. Officer Cox even showed me videos of Aries chasing people down and it was super cool to see. For such a badass name, Aries sure was a badass dog.

My favorite part of the entire ride-along happened to be the last stop we had. We had a call from a teen that had called 911 because her father had taken her phone away. I won't badmouth any of the two sisters that I got the opportunity to talk to and attempt to calm down but it was honestly the most fun I had during the entire ride-along. The best part was one of them asking for my Snapchat before we left.

Needless to say, I really enjoyed my experience not just with my ride-along but my time interviewing the other police officers as well. All of them were super kind to me and took time out of their day to share stories with me about their lives. My main goal was to make a strong positive impact for our police community, but they really made an impact on me. It was a pleasure getting to know these officers and I hope they truly know how grateful myself and others are for doing the job they do. Their stories were not all easy to share, but I am glad they gave me the opportunity to share them with the people who read this book so they truly know what our police go through on a daily basis.

My police story: Southport Chief of Police Thomas Vaughn

I grew up on the southside of Indianapolis, so it's kinda neat I'm the police chief of the same place I grew up. I went to St. Roch in elementary school up until I went to Perry Meridian middle school; I graduated from Perry. I had a mom and dad in the household. My dad was a police officer and also a marine. We had a good, what I would call average, life growing up, you know. We played sports, had family values, and had both parents in the house which I think makes a huge difference in the way you're raised. It was a really good childhood and I had a great life.

Before I joined, I actually went to Central 9 to be an auto mechanic, so I worked for a couple of auto parts places and ran their maintenance areas and sold parts. After that, I worked as a warehouse worker for a cold storage warehouse, and then from there, I went to the sheriff's department in Marion County and started my law enforcement career.

You know, I always thought it was just a really cool job. I used to always watch my dad get dressed up in uniform, put all his stuff on, and actually go out and do it. So probably from the time I was 10 or 11, I knew that was what I wanted to do; it was always my goal. Hearing their stories and watching a lot of the good things they did really motivated me.

My first day, I thought I was gonna solve all the world's problems and there was gonna be no crime. Now I kinda look at it as "OK, can we make a dent today?" The funny thing about my career that I can talk about is I had a big passion to serve at the beginning, and you go through this is my 26th year so you get into the middle part where you kinda lose faith that you're doing anything productive, and you're not solving all those. So, I worked for the City of Indianapolis for 20 years, well 18 years retired there, and became the police chief, so this is my 8th year as a police chief. And I still have that same drive and that same passion, I just look at it a lot different. To me, it's more as a patrolman starting out, it was arresting bad guys and doing that kinda stuff, and now it's more "How can we help them before they become bad guys?". So what kinda things can we do to implement that. Like, we have a whole support service here that does nothing but give back to the community, do events, we do fundraising events for kids with cancer. So how can we help these families not struggle so they're not out stealing and doing that kind of stuff. So, I would say that's the biggest thing from day one till now.

The most traumatic moment of my career was Lieutenant Aaron Allan being killed in 2017. I've been involved in seven police action shootings where the police officer died, but that one I was the chief, and I worked with him for days.

A lot of my job is working with the business owners and community people, churches and that kind of stuff. As the police chief, I can have those meetings where I sit down and we work through problems and we can come up with solutions to what they're going through. And then that opens the door to talk to that group of people. Last week alone, I talked to the Indian Muslim Coalition and then the Nigerian Muslim Coalition. I also met with Chin leaders. And then a couple of religious churches, but getting that different culture and all those, you learn a lot of different things about what their struggles are, how they were raised, and that kind of stuff. So, you know, just building those partnerships to where, you know, let's say we have somebody who's struggling and they don't have a place to live and they happen to be Muslim, I have all those contacts now to where I can reach out and be able to help them get a place to stay or get a job and that kind of stuff. So building those relationships are the core of what we do and what I think should be done. A lot of my job as police chief is being an ambassador for the police department or the city. I do a lot of community meetings where we talk about the events or the stuff we're doing trying to curb crime. So mine's more communicating with the community on what we're actually doing, not so much doing the making sure you've got ten patrolmen and that kind of stuff; that's more for my assistant chief and my deputy chief. We usually have a meeting everyday with the mayor to catch him up on what's happening from the last meeting. Today, I had a meeting with the sheriff. We have three excluded cities inside Marion county and then two towns we all meet and we talk about crime waves, things we've seen on the south side versus the north side, and come up with solutions on how to fix those. Last week, I had a regional meeting where we brought in all the ones from the counties around us. So a lot of my job is communication, passing information back and forth, that we can use to help us here.

17 years ago we went to a house that was on fire and we pulled out two kids that were stuck in the upper second story which was really I don't wanna say exciting but just the sense that you're saving a life was pretty cool that I remember a lot. I was involved in a police action shooting in 2001 where we were chasing a guy who was robbing hotels and he tried to kill himself and he hit a concrete barrier and the car caught on fire. So I went over, broke the window, and I pulled him out of the car. When I did, he pushed me away, reached back in the car and grabbed what we thought was a gun at the time. It turned out to be a tire iron and went like this with it, so I shot him twice, another officer shot him twice. We then went back up, pulled away from the burning car and were able to put pressure on his wounds and he actually lived through that. I've saved several with Narcan that have overdosed. One of the bad things about this job is that you never get to see the good sides of everybody, all the interactions are bad. My 2nd day in the police department, I was called to a crash, and they rear ended another car, and then they said a person was struck and I'm thinking "Well, how'd a person get struck?". When we got there, a mother was in the passenger seat, and she was holding an 8 month old baby, and when the husband rear ended the car, the baby went through the front windshield; then another car drove over it going the other way. And that was my 2nd 3rd day on the job, so you know you just see a lot of bad stuff that haunts you.

Life at home is hard. I've really tried I'm lucky, in June I'll have been married for 35 years; I married my high school sweetheart, we've had 3 kids and 4 grandkids but the other day we were at a volleyball game for my granddaughter and one guy gets in a pursuit, ends up in a crash, my phone goes off. Last night it went off at 1:30 and 4:00 in the morning, so you're constantly... you can't be 100% involved at what's going on at home, it always seems there's something that pulls you away. One of the things that I've tried to do is like, my wife and I have date nights on Friday nights, so for 3 hours I don't carry my phone, it's the assistant chief's job to take care of that. But it's always a constant you know if you work a business you work 8 hours and you don't think about that business no more my business is 24 hours a day, 7 days a week, that I always have somebody out there with a gun, in a car, putting their life on the line saving other lives. It never ends, you know? It's not like I can go to bed, close my eyes, and just not worry about what happens that night. There's always something that keeps you going.

People do thank us. It's usually when we're at a restaurant or doing something, people will come up and say thank you, we believe in you, and we still support you. I would say over the last two years with all the hate towards police that we've been thanked more and I think that's just those silent voices that want you to know that they still care about you.

My police story: Jordan Potee

I was born in Terre Haute, Indiana, but we moved up here when I was about six and I have lived up the southeast side my whole life. I played lots of cops and robbers with friends. I didn't play a whole lot of video games back then like a lot of my friends were. It was a big thing back then, like it is today, but even now I am not that into it. I mostly rode bikes into the park and mostly played cops and robbers in my free time. I always wanted to be a cop. When I was the bad guy from time to time I acted like the world was ending. It really started though when my parents were watching "Cops." I watched the police run around, save people, and take people to jail and that is when I started to get really into it. As I got older, I knew that I was going to do anything I could to get involved with law enforcement and get the bigger picture. I started out in the Explorers and aged out and became a civilian advisor to mentor the younger children who came in. Then, they had community volunteer police which I got into and then accident investigations before getting into Southport in February of 2021.

In high school, I worked at Kroger as a produce clerk. I was part-time until I graduated. When I graduated high school I started working full time and did that for about three years. I got hired as a special police officer in the department of coding for four and a half years and that is when I took a job as a public safety officer which is mainly special police. We were just civilian accident investigators.

A good amount of your first few years, you are learning. It is a bit overwhelming at times, but also still a lot of positives because this is it. This is real life, not on TV, not in an Explorer trying to understand the concept, you are not a civilian volunteer, you are the actual police. At the start is the academy, which is the first six months of your career. If you go to a law enforcement academy it is three and a half months. A large 6 months of that is field training before you get cut loose.

A lot of it is mental and physical from day 1 to the last day. A good amount of it is classroom and another good amount is physically hands-on using that training and what you learned in the classroom into physical work. Most important ones though are criminal law and traffic law. Those are the two longest parts of the academy but absolutely the most important things to learn.

This is not only where tons of friendships are made, but one of the biggest families that you will ever join nationwide. You will establish tons of friendships but a small bit of those friendships actually become family relationships. My lieutenant here is one of my supervisors. We have known each other a little bit before that but then just as he has watched me go through these steps and go into the academy, FTO, and now we work together and it is incredible. We have a strong relationship and it is awesome how we've grown. In my home life, honestly with me and my dad our relationship has improved. My dad is a sports fanatic, so me being the first born he expected me to do sports. I did not do sports. As he has seen me grow older and he understands the job more and it is not just the stuff you see on TV, like he used to, family life is good and it is very supportive. You want supportive family members and supportive friends. I have a good "off- switch" when I get home and you need to have that or you are never gonna get a break from this job. A lot of times if you do not get a break from this job, it is one of the most draining mentally and physically jobs you could ever have.

There is at least one person everyday that I will hear a thank-you from. This may shock you but I personally receive more thank-yous than I actually receive hate. Now obviously each day is different so some days we are getting people that do not like us but there is actually a large amount of people now and I hear it at least once a day.

My police story: Brandon Cox

I grew up in Franklin. My dad is a sheriff's deputy and still is and then I have my mom. She worked at a couple different places. She worked at Ford for a long time. I have an older brother who's four years older than me who graduated from Indiana University, and he works for an insurance company now, and then there's me. I grew up in Franklin and graduated from Franklin High School. I have two uncles and two other cousins that are police officers. One uncle works here as a Johnson County sheriff's deputy. My other uncle worked for the agency near Dallas as a police officer. One of my cousins is still a Whiteland police officer and then another one is a police officer in Irving, Texas, so close to Dallas. I was pretty normal, played sports and played baseball mainly. I grew up in a strict home but nothing too crazy.

I was in the Marine Corps for nine years. I did active duty the whole time. In high school, I had a couple regular jobs. I worked as a groundskeeper for the parks department, and did stuff like that, but nothing too serious until I joined the Marine Corps. I turned 18 in October of 2006 and graduated from high school at midterm so I graduated in December of '06. January 2nd I left for bootcamp for the Marine Corps.

Police work is something I've wanted to do my entire life. Especially watching my dad and my uncles. Just kinda grew up in the *COPS* T.V. show era. So I was the kid that had my own little gun belt and would play cop around the neighborhood all the time. I never wanted to be the bad guy, I always wanted to be the cop, so that had a lot to do with it. It was just kinda my time to get out of the Marine Corps. I would've stayed in, but it was always in the back of my mind that I wanted to do this. So it was kinda that time, you know, being 10 years in, where you either stay until retirement or get out and do something different. By that time I was 26-27, so I put in a couple of different applications here and there and just had the mindset of "if it was meant to be it'll happen". With Greenwood specifically, the whole hiring process, I was able to take leave to come home because I was stationed in California the whole time. And it just so happened to be times where I could come home and do different parts of the hiring process and everything. And then literally like two weeks before I had to make the decision whether to reenlist or get out, Greenwood called and said "Hey, we're gonna hire you." so I ended up getting out in June of 2015.

I would say obviously the political environment is a lot different now, not necessarily from the beginning, it kinda comes and goes you know? I think there's a lot more scrutiny on law enforcement than when I first started which is for good and bad reasons. Some of it's good, some of it's bad. But as far as the job, it's always kinda been the same. The job never changes, it's always just kinda more the environment we're policing in is what changes, but it never really changes. What people think we do or what people think we should do or what people think about how we do things all those things change, but the job again, I think will always stay the same. You know technology changes the way we do certain things. But yeah at the end of the day it's the same thing: you're catching bad guys and helping people. I mean it's kinda what we do; it's different than what my dad and my uncles and stuff, you know the environment, but they were still doing the same things that we do now.

The most mentally challenging thing has to be anything involving children. Especially the very young kids who, you know, are completely helpless in certain situations like car accidents, parents overdosing and dying; they don't really know what's going on. I've seen parents of kids die in car crashes and very young kids in the back of ambulances with their mom getting CPR as she's dying in the ambulance. Especially having a son, it didn't really bother me before having a son, but now that I'm a parent it's hard not to see those children and immediately think of my son. You know, obviously you sympathize with kids in really terrible situations, but you always just think "God forbid that was my child". You kinda relate to them in kind of a different way once you have kids of your own. I think it's that way with anybody, especially with kids being in terrible situations is gonna affect everyone, and with the things we see everyday, whether it be car accidents, people in bad situations, people making bad parenting choices, alcohol has a lot to do with it, drug overdoses, situations where the kid is pretty much helpless. I wouldn't call it traumatizing, but would say it's mentally probably the hardest thing to deal with on a daily basis. There've been a couple situations where I've turnaquetted people from gunshot wounds and stuff like that. Gotten people from really bad domestic situations where they would've been seriously hurt or injured had we not gotten there at the right time. I've probably narcanned like twelve people by now. Yeah, I would say just the medical emergencies and things like are the most common things that stick out to me.

We only deal with people on the worst days of their life, and you see someone who's in a very bad situation whether you're arresting them or getting them help and then you see them a couple years later and barely recognize them and they walk up to you and go "Hey, do you remember me?" You're like "Holy Crap, wow ok" and they've turned their life around. It doesn't happen every time like that. Sometimes you see them and they're worse off. I always think that's really cool especially with the drugs and alcohol stuff. People can go down a really bad road and then end up recovering from it and then you see them and they're like "Hey I appreciate you for not judging me and being respectful. You know I've turned my life around; I've got this kid now, I've got a job." You know, whatever it is they've got going on now it's pretty cool to see. And then relationship wise, especially being with the dog, I've gotten to train with different agencies and people from different backgrounds; got to train with a bunch of special forces guys. So having a dog, specifically on the drug side of things, you have that tool, as we'll call him, that's gonna find it for you. There are other ways, obviously there are exceptions on searching vehicles and stuff like that. But he's the instant probable cause tool. So he's great to have especially for that kind of stuff. But the biggest thing is the amount of stuff he deters just from his presence. If anybody's near the car, they know he's there. You pull up on a call and everybody sees K9 people are gonna be less likely to get belligerent with you when they know that he's back there and he's a factor. But that being said too, I've had people look right at him and run away, but that's like "You're not gonna outrun the dog". That's the thing too, if someone decides to run and hide, I've got the hide-and-seek champion in the backseat who's gonna come find you. I won't say he makes things easier. It's a lot of constant training; I'm with him more than I am my son because the dog lives with me, the dog goes to work with me, my son doesn't go to work with me. He farts in my car, I have to deal with his dog hair, grooming and things like that. It's basic stuff with a dog, but imagine having a dog in your car for 12 hours at a time. But, he's also like my best friend so there's the work aspect of it and then there's the companionship of it where you do spend that much time with an animal and the bond is like none other. It's funny because he can sense my moods, I can sense his moods, like when I'm cranky he can tell, when he's cranky I can tell. It's just funny that we can kinda feel each other out. But as far as the police work side of it goes, it is amazing to watch them. You can have someone run, and then we can show up 5 minutes after this person's run, and he'll put his nose to the ground and find that person a half a mile away from where they started. It's pretty amazing. And then the other part, it doesn't have to be people running from the police, we've had people wander away from nursing homes, people with dementia and stuff like that. It's the same thing, I mean human odor is human odor. They're still gonna find you regardless of what you've done or the reason why we're looking for you. So, they just bring a whole different dynamic. And the interesting thing about it too, people think of police dogs and they just think "oh, they're just these vicious animals". Like, no. The dog cuddles my fiance at home. He's not some rabid, bloodthirsty creature.

In any police department you're gonna have people from totally different backgrounds; that was the best part about the military: all my best friends when I was in were from completely different backgrounds from what I experienced, all different places, life experiences. I had friends that were legitimate gang members and had gotten into trouble and the military was the only way out. I had friends that were completely sheltered and from really small towns, I had friends from different countries where English was their second language. You had people from Mexico, just people from all different places, which was really cool. It's kinda the same in the police department because most of them are decent size; you have 60-70 people with different backgrounds. So that's always cool.

I would say everyday at work at least one person will either honk and wave at me or just come up and say thanks; especially around here. I would say more people will show outward respect versus outward disrespect. You still get people that make a certain hand gesture to you or say something to you, but it's more often than not when you walk inside a business or someone's house or whatever, they'll thank you or buy you lunch or whatever the case may be.

My police story: Dawn Asbury

I grew up in a divorced home, but both of my parents were very active in my life. They couldn't stay together married, but they were amazing parents. I was taught a strong work ethic and good moral ethic code. Both of my parents worked really hard to make sure I got whatever I needed. As much as they didn't like each other, they still got along when it came to me. It was a pretty good childhood. My mom worked really hard and put herself through college and she was an Indianapolis Public Schools teacher for 32 years and she just retired. Dad worked at the same job for 37 years. We went on vacation and had fun. I had a really easy, fun childhood so I do not have many complaints at all.

I have been a nanny, a daycare worker, a preschool teacher, a parts buyer for a machine shop, a marketing director for a Fortune 500 company, a leasing agent for an apartment complex, a manager for an apartment complex, and I have worked at a bar and restaurant. I have been doing a lot of things. I met my husband and he was a police officer when we met and that is how I got into it. I actually met my husband at the apartment complex I was working at and he came for a courtesy officer job and I just thought he was the bees knees. It was a Saturday and I was in the office by myself, and I heard the door chimes and I was actually putting on makeup because I was running late. I looked up and saw him and I pretty much knew right then and there he was it. I have made a lot of new friends. Being a police officer a lot of people do not understand what you really do and what you deal with, so you get really close to your peers. We would love for people to try and understand but no one wants to because they don't care. Which is okay, that is their choice.

I am definitely not as naive to the world as I was before I met my husband and became a police officer. My understanding is better than what it was before. You are so naive to stuff that happens that you don't know about. You don't understand that there are so many things that are happening that you don't know about because people take care of it before it comes your direction. I was a very naive person until I became a police officer. That is for sure.

I have had a rape case with a 6 year old girl. From overdoses, to kids choking, to suicides and talking people out of that. I have done a couple of those. Those probably get to you the most, especially when it is kids. I met a kid in the parking lot of a high school with a knife and it was over his grades. He thought he was disappointing his parents with his grades and that was rough. I stood out there with him in the rain for an hour and a half and I talked to him and hugged him. I think the advantage I have is that I am a mother of four. That gives me an advantage with parents and kids because of the mom mentality. It is easier to talk to people when you are a mom.

We get thank-yous all the time. It is very much appreciated but sometimes it feels awkward. It is nice to know that some people still care a little bit, but at the same time I know at least myself and a few others are not doing it for the thanks we just want to help. I do not want to be on the news every time I save someone. That 10 minutes of helping someone is all that matters even if it is just you and that one person. We don't need 50 other people taking pictures of me, like thank you it is appreciated but, as long as that person knows that I am there and I am doing it for them then it makes my whole career.

My police story: Interviewee wishes to remain anonymous.

I grew up in Center Gove. My parents still live in the same house actually, so I never moved. My father is a machinist. My mother works at FedEx. I don't know exactly what she does there but has been there for about twenty-five years. I would really say that my upbringing was just awesome. My parents were very supportive. They were strict, but supportive in almost anything I wanted to do. We had dinner every night at the same time and so we're very organized. I can say they made sure that you know my education always came first and then sports. I mean I can sum it up by saying it was just an awesome childhood.

So when I was in high school I worked at Wendy's and places like that. When 9/11 happened, I was actually going to Butler on a college visit and when it happened that day and I don't know what it was, but it was like okay I know what I'm going to do now. I am strictly military. I have a grandpa that was in the Army and a couple other cousins and stuff that were in the Army, but I went to the Marine Corps. I graduated four months later. I spent four and a half years from the end of ‘03 to the middle of ‘08 and had three deployments to Iraq. I was a sniper for the Marine Corps and eventually I got out as a Sergeant. After that I worked at Community Corrections and it is kinda funny because my wife had the power of an attorney. On my last deployment Greenwood Police Department was hiring, so she pretty much was able to fill out all the paperwork for me legally and submit my packet. So that was my plan, to get out of the military and then I wanted to be a cop. I got out and a day or two later I got a letter in the mail saying that my packet was denied because my wife forgot to submit a birth certificate. She felt horrible for that and I said that everything happens for a reason and I live by that. I got a job at Johnson County Community Corrections which is right next to the jail. It is a work-related home detention program. I was a corrections officer there for a couple of years and Greenwood began another hiring process. I submitted my application, was accepted and that was in August of 2011.

I joined the police force because I knew a detective that worked for Greenwood. I was in between my 2nd and 3rd deployment, and I got to come home for 10 days. In those 10 days, I went out with that detective and three more of them. Two of them were in narcotics, so they had beards and long hair and they did not look like police. We were sitting there eating at El Meson and one of those guys picked up their phone and was talking to a drug dealer. He was like "Hey, I'll be there in a few minutes." I was just in shock. That really impacts the community. Drugs just breed crimes. They are the main reason for burglaries because people are just stealing things to sell and buy drugs. In my head I knew that was what I wanted to do. I couldn't tell you the year but it was July 18th when I decided that when I finished up my time in the military, I wanted to get out and be in the police department and be with the narcotics. I was able to do that within six years and I have been there ever since and I absolutely love it.

It is like anything new. I think the police department's kind of paramilitary so they have rank structure and stuff like that, so I was used to that but learning all the laws and new people at once and stuff and learning my responsibilities here is just the same thing I mean with any other job I think. I was nervous. Then about a year, maybe two into the job you start to not be as nervous, you begin to understand the job more, and you understand that you can talk to almost anybody and get them to stand down. You don't always have to put your hands on people. There are times for that. I learned that pretty quick in my career. There's a bunch of officers that taught me that talking is a lot easier and it's more beneficial to both parties to talk someone down rather than being hands-on. I would say that I hope I try to learn every day just like I was there the day 1. So I mean there's something I told my kids, my wife and my kids especially to learn something new everyday. And so far I have done that. Everyday I'll see an officer, whether older or newer, but they'll say something and I'll be like "Oh my gosh, that is so much easier that way." or "I have been doing this wrong for a while."

The most traumatic thing was probably about seven years ago. The guys in uniform, the guys that work the road, they got a call. I was a general detective at this time and that just means that I have no specialties. I pretty much go to any place that they sent to me. A lot of thefts, robberies, things like that and I was getting pretty good at those. Anyway, the road gets called on a welfare check in a very small home. It was actually a double and they went in there. I was getting ready to leave to go home and I heard on the radio that they had requested a detective. So I went out there and I saw a man who was probably 70 to 73 years old with one leg and he weighed roughly 85 lbs. The welfare check started by a neighbor seeing an older man knocking on a window saying "help help." Knowing everything now, what had happened was the man's wife had kept him in a room for about a year and a half. He was only fed Meals on Wheels which is like a school lunch, only worse. He had one Meals on Wheels meal a day and a 2 liter bottle of Pepsi for a year-and-a-half. The guy was a veteran, so his wife was taking any kind of money he was getting from the government on that side of it and he had been in this room for a year-and-a-half. There was a pile of used adult diapers in this room and at one point when you walk up on the outside it looks like dirt is all over the window. When you go inside the room it was flies covering the window. So eventually, I talked to the man and he had told us that for the past eight months he'd try to sleep at night, but he would have to put his blanket over his head so the flies wouldn't bother him and he could sleep. And that was really hard to see. Like unfortunately I've seen some see some things overseas that you know aren't good either, but that was the closest thing I could really see to torture. I just couldn't believe that one person could do that to another, especially a husband and wife that loved each other and stuff like that. I'm not going to say it was really traumatic for me to see but I think about him a lot still. His wife has since passed. He lives with his daughter now, and he gained like 85 lbs in a couple months. I mean he is just living life. I see his daughter every once in a while in a restaurant we go to and we talk for a little bit, but he's doing great. He's a big guy, he's a big New England fan which is alright, I guess. But I mean that would also be kind of like my most rewarding case because I was able to file charges on her abuse.

Before I worked at Greenwood I was a Reserve officer in Trafalgar for a year. A Reserve officer is basically a cop but you don't get paid. I'm getting ready for my second night on the job and I'm riding with an officer who says "Hey, there's a bad accident down here we need to get down there and help." So we leave and we go up there, and when we got there that was the first time I've ever seen somebody killed due to a car accident. The lady was obese and was driving a Cadillac CTS that was silver, but the seatbelt damn near cut her head off. And I was expecting to go up there and help a person get out of a vehicle, but instead I was like "woah" when we got to the scene. I also don't know if I've ever seen in a car accident, a car look like that afterward. I have seen trucks and other vehicles in explosions and stuff like that but I've never seen a car damaged like that before. It was a truck and the CTS and they rammed head on and everyone in the truck was just fine and walked out but she didn't.

I met my wife sophomore year in European history at Center Grove. I always tell people that she was the one copying off of me, but that is entirely not true. We started dating our senior year. After prom and graduation she knew I was going into the Marines. She went to Ohio State and I went to the Marines. We were able to see each other every couple of months in between deployments. I would fly her out for the weekend or on a long weekend and we made it work. We have such a good relationship and I'll tell all the guys about it. You know how guys talk sometimes, but I am always like I am so happy with my wife and my family it is unreal. As far as people in the department, I do not want to say I have a best friend, but Sergeant Brian Folco is just one of those guys you are drawn to. I was in the department for about three years and I was given a nickname, amongst many, but it was "Universal Bro" and that was just because I got along with everybody. I try to teach my kids that too. There is not enough time to hate anybody or not to be friends with people because you always have something in common with somebody. I would say I have close to ten good relationships here in the department with seventy-one working here. There are my really close friends but we all kinda hang out together. At Greenwood, you have road officers that are in the black and white police cars and they know on day one, January 1st, they know what hours they are working on what days because they are scheduled all throughout the year. Then you have detectives, who have more freedom and you can plan out your week accordingly based on how many cases you are working. So if I have interviews scheduled on certain days, I can kinda make my schedule on that rather than working a nine to five everyday. More so what I do in narcotics, I work when drug dealers work. More times than I like to admit, but I'll tell my wife I am home for dinner, and then sometimes I'll get a call and I gotta go do my job. It is good on the back end though because I only work so many hours a month. If I work a 17 hour day, then I might not work at all the next day or only work a few hours. If I work a ton of hours in the first three weeks of the month then sometimes in the last week of the month I may not have to work because I hit all of my hours already, so that can be handy at times. It is a lot harder, as a detective, to not bring stuff home. I am always thinking of the stuff I have to do tomorrow, whether that's an interview, a meeting, a search warrant, or something like that. Road guys can go six to six and that would be it for the day. We like to say the road guys get what they can do in the twelve hour shift, and what they don't get done we get to finish it. Both jobs are difficult, they are just difficult differently. I would say though, it is hard not to bring stuff home.

Every morning, my routine is to start making the coffee, wake up the kids and get them going for school, and hop in the shower. While I am in the shower I am thinking about what I have planned for the day, so I do think about it more at home. There is about a thirty minute period when I get home, my kids always ask questions and they're young, both under ten years old, a boy and a girl, and they always want to know whether or not daddy got the bad guy or not. I say yeah, but I make sure they understand that just because I arrested a person the day before that they aren't necessarily a bad person they just made a mistake. I try not to take it home, but it does happen. My wife is really good at handling it, she is amazing.

We have a huge, supportive community. In my capacity right now, since I do not look like a police officer, not as much as others, but yes. Chick-Fil-A is incredible. Just last week they brought in tons and tons of sandwiches for us. We will have random people who live in the city bring in tons of stuff like donuts, which is kinda stereotypical, but cake pops and Gatorades, and a lady even brought in like fifteen cases of Monster energy drinks. It is amazing the amount of support we have around here. Johnson County as a whole, they appreciate us. When I worked in the D.E.A. (Drug Enforcement Administration), federal agencies can borrow officers by paying overtime and the department receives a direct line to those agencies. There is a lot of red tape to get federal agency help on a lot of things, but if you have an officer working for one of those agencies, you have a direct line to the agencies and request help in an easier way. When I worked for that, I was in Indianapolis the majority of the time, and it was a very thankless job up there.

My police story: Cody Robertson

I grew up in Greenwood, Indiana and I went to Northeast Elementary. I went to Greenwood Middle School and then to Greenwood High School, so I was in Greenwood my entire adolescent life. I lived with both my parents. I had a pretty good childhood; always out riding bicycles and playing basketball and football. I played football, basketball, and baseball all through my freshman year of high school.

Growing up my dad had friends that worked for IMPD (Indianapolis Metropolitan Police Department) at the time, and their work always kinda interested me. When I turned eighteen, I did a ride along and seeing how the officers interacted with the community really drew me to wanting to be a part of that. The way the community interacted with officers is like the town of Mayberry. Everyone waves to you, everyone says hello, and they know they can call on you and you will be attentive to their needs. As far as going beyond doing actual police work, we are really big on community policing. That can be as simple as waving to everybody as you drive past, and we've shoveled driveways for people in the winter when there's no runs out. We pull trash cans up for elderly people, we bring groceries in. I mean you name it, we try to do it. We want people to know that we are here to help. We took an oath to protect and serve. We have done really, really well on the protection part,and now we're working hard for the serve part. We try to balance everything out.

Before I was a police officer, I was an auto mechanic. I worked on every vehicle that had diesel engines. I was an ASE certified mechanic.

For my first day, I started in the police academy, and it was in July of 2014. I have never ever been in an environment like that. It was very structured. Even more structured than school. There's tons of running, tons of physical training involved, and even on my first run I was as nervous as you can be even doing something as routine as stopping a car. Now my speciality is

K9 and criminal investigations. I am the lieutenant of the K9 Criminal Investigations Unit. My dog barks a lot. He is excellent at finding narcotics or missing people, or someone who ran from the police. It is also good for public relations. He is pretty social. He can go from doing a dope search and finding a suspect to letting a little kid pet him. It is good to have him to intermingle with the community as well.

I am a lieutenant over criminal investigations for the Southport police department and I am an officer, as well, for the Perry Township school police. I am primarily assigned to Perry Meridian High School. Our days start out kinda like being an older brother. I start out my morning saying "Good morning, how are you doing" to everyone I see. The response you get from that is great. You build a rapport so if a situation is happening they will come up to you. It can be something like "My parents were arguing last night." and we talk about it with them. I always say we get what we give, so if I am very upfront and nice to them I get guys I can have a full conversation with that I probably wouldn't get to if I wasn't inside the school. I get to know different people and different walks of life. In Perry Township, we are one of the most diverse school districts in the State of Indiana. I believe we have like 93 different nationalities that are from various parts of the country. You get to know all their customs, their culture, and I have tried a ton of different food that I probably would not get to try anywhere else.

As a police officer, I have responded to several vehicle crashes. In one, a guy was having a heart attack while he was driving. We thought we were just responding to a normal vehicle crash but when we got there he was in cardiac arrest in the driver's seat of the vehicle. We pulled him out and started CPR on him and got him an AED which our cars are equipped with, and was able to continue CPR until the paramedics arrived to take over. The guy ended up making it and survived and walked out of the hospital a week later.

On July 27th of 2017 my partner was killed in the line of duty. It was lieutenant Aaron Allan. He responded to a vehicle that was overturned and he was shot multiple times. It was less than a half mile from where we are now.

There are some certain times and runs that will affect you for the rest of your day and the rest of your life. Losing my partner in 2017, there are still times that I miss him like crazy.

Aaron was like a brother to me. Being at home, though, makes me appreciate my time at home more. I realized how fortunate myself and my family are to live the way that we do. That is one of the biggest takeaways from that. It makes you very, very grateful for your family because you see a lot of people on their worst days. You have to keep that in mind and have a switch in a situation where someone needs help changing a tire on a road, to responding to a robbery in progress. You have to flip a switch and bring another side of you out. You have to prepare for whatever you are going to roll up on. It is the aspect of not knowing what you're pulling up on. So even though it could be a crash, like with the man in cardiac arrest. I went in fully expecting to see a crash with a vehicle fully off the road that struck a power pole. It was not. It was someone in cardiac arrest, so you have to be able to think very rapidly. We are trained in crisis intervention for someone who could be having a medical or psychiatric crisis. We have to be able to change our thinking as a situation is evolving.

I have made a lot of new relationships with community members. I try to treat everyone with dignity and respect. No matter whether I am taking a man to jail or a lady is flagging me down to say hello. I treat everyone with the same level of respect. Based on that you will have people you have never met in any other aspect of your life that are friendly to you and will come to you if they need help. You can be pumping gas at the gas station and people will come up and thank us for serving and what we do. I have guys thank me when I have taken them to jail. Just last night we served a search warrant on a house and the guy was sitting there and he said "Even though I have done some bad things, you have never treated me bad." That really stuck out because I always say it is a bad day, not a bad life. I do not treat someone differently based on something they did on one day. Treating people with respect is something that we owe to the community and the community thanks us for it. You meet people from all different walks of life.

My police story: Brian Folco

My mom was a school teacher and my dad was a cop. My mom taught German and English. Dad was on Indianapolis Police Department until he got Bell's palsy and retired for a little while and got back into the police work serving warrants with the Marion County Justice Agency, FTA (failure to appear in court), and did felony warrants. We grew up until 6th grade in Perry Township in Marion County where dad worked and we moved to the Center Grove area in 7th grade in '88 or somewhere around there. That was a little different. I mean losing all your friends and moving from one school district to another one, it was completely separate. So I had to make new friends and new buddies.It was a healthy environment. I had both parents and they cared and wanted us to go to school, but of course I didn't. I joined the Marine Corps. It was a good childhood. For fun, I was always out with my buddies riding dirt bikes and just ran around together until everybody got driver licenses and there was a place called Dell's Billiards there in town right behind Kroger on Meridian Park Drive. It was kinda the local hangout. Then we'd go four wheeling out in Atterbury and just stuff that didn't cause anybody any trouble. Then I joined the Marine Corps two days after I graduated high school and was in San Diego. That's pretty much my childhood and my friends and I left most of my buddies and kept in touch with just a few from high school.

When I got home from the Marines I got into a construction job right away. A couple of days later I was in construction with a friend of mine, Joey Rodriguez, and he ended up getting me into the police work in the end. So I started that, got into a plumbing apprenticeship working for Rodriguez Enterprises and his name was Chad Paulen. I went to school playing football with his brother, so I knew of Chad but I didn't know him well till we started working together. He offered me the apprenticeship and I had done that and applied for the Chrysler Founder in between. So I was working for Chad Paulen for probably two years or so as a plumber's apprentice before Chrysler called and I was out there for 11 years in the Chrysler

Founder and made cast-iron engine blocks for all Chrysler stuff and ended up being the people operator out there. I was in charge of making all the iron for production, so I will get everything set up for the third shift and get ready for the production runs on days and afternoon shifts. I did that until it closed down and of course, we had Shane, my son, during that period of time and I ended up taking a buyout and I worked for another construction company called JDC that was Chad Peters, the guy who was the best man at my wedding. I worked for them for a brief period of time maybe a year and IPL was calling looking for a lot of his foundry guys because there's not a lot of difference between making foundry iron believe it or not, so I started out there and had applied for Greenwood Police Department in between and I was an IPL for probably close to a year. Then all of a sudden here comes the phone call for being a cop and that's what I've been doing since then.

I started out as a patrolman and ran a district. I was in charge of the west side of Greenwood. I didn't have any other responsibilities other than taking runs. Short time after that, I was asked to join the Special Weapons And Tactics (SWAT) team because of my military background. So I started on the SWAT team and about that same period of time I got firearms and general instructor and went to school for that. I took a patrol rifle instructor course and they really geared me towards taking all that over since I was in the infantry in the Marine Corps. So I really got to do a lot of things that I had as career goals pretty early. I actually thought I wanted to be a K-9 officer but the more you're around those guys you see the dog is a lot of commitment and there is a lot of dirt. They are constantly trying to keep their cars clean, so while I really enjoyed being around the dogs, I decided that was probably not something that I was going to do. I ended up being a SWAT team leader and a sniper on the SWAT team and ended up being the sniper team leader. I retired from that almost two years ago now. I got to do a lot of the things I wanted to do career wise pretty early. I did ten years on the SWAT team, and about a year and a half ago we had an admin change with a new chief and he asked me to be the training coordinator so I do all the training for the department and take care of all the training. I get those young cops. It is part of what I do is start them out and get them involved in the training. First I ask them "Why are you here?" because if they aren't in that service oriented mindset but say something like they want to lock people up. I have not had someone say that to me but it is very much stay focused on you are here to help. There is a misconception that you pay your own salary, and while there is some truth to that, we are out there to maintain the laws of the nation and the state of Indiana and that is a big responsibility. I tell them to stay updated on the law because it constantly changes. I get updates on my computer and I personally send them out myself to officers. I also say to not lose sight of why you're here.

The department is very much a camaraderie. You are going places other people wouldn't and facing dangers other people normally would walk away from or run away from. So that brings you together and bonds you together. The Black Lives Matter movement and a lot of the anti-police movement stuff like that has helped bond everyone in the department. It was us against them kinda thing for a long time in the public eye, but I got to say the City of Greenwood as a whole rallied around us during that time too. We got a lot of cookies and support letters and things like that, so it was definitely worse for other agencies. But that kind of backlash when you're just trying to do your job tends to unify, and of course, you're making relationships that are lifelong friendships. On the veteran side, a lot of us tend to flock together. I was the only Marine when I got hired on and now there are six of us. There are quite a few soldiers and sailors and three or four airmen. So that previous bond brings everyone together on that end of things but outside of that you're friends with people that have never served before, and some of my best friends are people that never served in anything. It goes back to that common bond of wanting to really serve the community.

You see the best and worst in people. Probably traffic accidents and some of the things you see during that. That's probably the most dramatic thing right off the bat, and it affects you the most because you just don't see stuff like that all the time. Some of those accidents can be pretty traumatic because of the things it can do to the human body and, of course, the sight and the smells, too. Some of the people are dead and some are alive and we try to help them get out of there without hurting them any further. I would say that is pretty traumatic.

There was a team of us that happened to be involved in a shooting. It was probably about a decade ago. I don't keep track of them, it's not something I like to hash and think about much. We went to a noise complaint and it ended up being a guy with a large stereo and long story short, he opened the door and took a shot at me. So when he shot at me and missed me, the bullet went across the hallway into the apartment door across from us. Now, initially if we didn't know anything past that, we were more worried about getting the guy out there without having to shoot him or him shooting us. As it turned out, the bullet that missed me actually hit a lady in the apartment across from us. A short time later she opened the front door and told me she had been shot. We had a barricaded gunman and this all happened within an eight foot or nine foot stretch, so the guy that shot at me and missed me was only about three feet away from me. He had closed the door and went back inside. We had to get the lady out because she was shot through the leg and started going into shock. Because I was on the SWAT team I was put in charge of that right away and got everybody set up to get her out. We ended up getting her out and, unfortunately, the gunman tried to get out too and ended up being killed in the process because he had raised his gun back up at a couple of the other police officers that I had put up on a corner. When he came out he had lived down the hallway that I had the lady out to get treated. I received the Medal of Valor for that and a few of the other guys did too. During the award ceremony that lady came and thanked us, too. It was a pretty emotional ceremony, and in that story I could say I had a direct effect in saving that woman's life since I was running the show, but unfortunately you're reacting to a lot of what someone else is doing too. Everything we did was set up in case he decided to come back out, which he ended up doing and he wanted to continue the gun fight. It was a bad situation, but at the same time we got to help an innocent bystander who wasn't part of the thing at all. I questioned if there was anything else we could've done to avoid it but the bottom line was he decided to come out and shoot at me. You never want to see a situation where someone could get hurt and a noise complaint is not something you expect to go that way, either. I have been involved in several other team situations where had we not acted, people probably would've been seriously injured or dead.

At home, I don't talk about it much and I don't focus on it that much. I mean neither did my dad. You could tell when he would come home he would need to unwind. I worked the night shift for the vast majority of my career, until I picked up the sergeant position. Even after that for a while I still worked nights but I had to come up with a program where you find the time to unwind too. For me, when I was on nights, I would make sure the kids got up and went to school and I would shower and unwind for the night. You have to leave work at work. You can't carry the stuff with you. I see the best in people and I see the worst in people and the worst in people can be pretty bad. If you're not careful you'll start looking at society differently and think that everyone is out there trying to get you or something. It's not like that and you have to keep that in mind and it is a constant balance. It is one of those things where if I had a bad day and I need some time, I will vocalize that. I try not to carry it home and I am not always successful but I would say most of the time I am especially the longer I do this. With training, I don't have to face the dangers a road officer does everyday. I am not out there taking runs everyday. I'll help them, but I am still in uniform most of the time. It is not like it was where I was waiting for something to go on the radio and I went in as a response. I go help out where help is needed, but it is very different now from what it used to be. There's a lot more pressure on me since I am more of an administrator now and part of the chain of command for the admin. And due to less and less of the Black Lives Matter movements and the other anti-police stuff it is not all in your face like it was months ago. I can honestly say that I do not know any racist officers and I know hundreds and hundreds of cops. Any cop that is racist is open about it. It is not cool and we don't look at it like that. We got a diverse, though not as diverse as other departments, but we got a diverse department with different ethnicities and males and females. It irritates those that are on the other side of it that are not caucasian males. Again, there is less of that now so it is not as big of a deal seeing it on the news all the time. On the other side of it, if a cop does something bad, it irritates the whole mess of us regardless if it is our department or another department. If they're doing something they know they are not supposed to do. It is a bad reflection on the profession.

We get thanked all the time. I took a run once on Thanksgiving and came back out to my car and there was a whole meal on the hood and a thank-you card on top. No signature but a thank-you card. People buy us dinners and buy us lunches. Good luck going through a fast food line without someone buying your lunch, especially in a marked car. It is also not uncommon for three or four of us to go to a sit-down restaurant and when we go up to pay the check, someone anonymously paid the check already.

My Police Story: Glen Folco

I grew up in a middle-class family in Sheboygan, Wisconsin. My father spent more money than he earned, so my mom had to scrape together to make ends meet. Life was rough so as soon as I could I left my childhood home. I joined the Marine Corps when I was 18.

I spent 3 years in the Marine Corps and was in Vietnam in '67 and '68. After Vietnam, I went to Lakeland College in Sheboygan, Wisconsin, and I graduated there in 3 years with summa cum laude. I came down to Indianapolis because some scholarships were available for me to get my master's degree. I had choices from Tulane, Ball State, and Butler. I took Butler because my wife was from Indianapolis and I could get a job with my father-in-law to help make ends meet. While in college, during the Summers, I would work digging ditches by hand for a gas company and they paid pretty good. Since I was paying for my own college, that helped a lot because the G.I. Bill didn't pay squat for Vietnam veterans. It is not like what it is today. I did construction work for my father-in-law and quickly became a supervisor. Unfortunately, he let his nephew run the company at the end and he ran the business into the ground, so I knew I had to leave and I did.

At that time in my life, I originally wanted to be a history professor, but I knew that was not going to happen. In the '70s, we had what was called the Rust Belt in the Midwest, where factories were closing and jobs were going overseas, and we had terrible inflation rates where sometimes it was at 14%. Due to that, colleges were not hiring and they were reducing staff, so getting a job as a college history professor was pretty much impossible.

I had to make a living, and a friend of mine got me interested in the police department. I applied to the Indianapolis, Marion County Sheriff's Department, and Indiana State Police. I waited a year and nothing happened. One month, I got acceptance from all three departments. I picked the Indianapolis Police Department because at the time they had a take-home car, a 10% college incentive, and very good insurance; plus I knew some people in the department.

We graduated from the academy on a Friday night, and they didn't pay overtime. They just paid you a salary. They put us on parade detail, race detail, and on Monday I reported to work in my district car. I was given an officer to ride with and we did basic police work. It was a pretty simple beginning.

During my first year, I was enthusiastic as hell, like everyone else. After that, you get beat around and the job changed. By the time I was 60, I was kinda ready to get out of the job, but more about that shortly.

When I first started out, we were the first graduating class to start with a radio. All we had on our belts were a batton, a flashlight, a gun, handcuffs and extra ammunition. Today, cops have so much stuff on their belts, that I don't even know how the hell they can walk around. We didn't have tasers, and I think they are used too much. We would manhandle people down without having to use one because when you use a taser on someone you have to charge them with resisting law enforcement. We didn't have to do that. We would just take them down and cuff them. We didn't have the cameras either. And the problem with the cameras is that they can give you the visual, but they can't give you the feel of the situation. After you have been on the street awhile, you can tell what is up by people's mannerisms and stuff. Most of the time, not all the time, because you can still always get fooled, on whether or not a guy was going to run or not, or turned ballistic or whatever, and you don't get that on a camera.

The first group I was assigned to had a bunch of good officers. We had a lot of fun. Most of us had shot people because back then, that was the way it went. I would party with them and be with them most of the time, but unfortunately, now most of them are dead. Policemen die early, why I don't really know. Stress, I guess. Currently, I meet monthly with some friends for breakfast, but unfortunately, my partner, George, passed away last Christmas. We are just getting old and some of us have too many medical problems, so it is hard to stay in touch with the old guys.

There were too many traumatic events during my career. I had to kill a guy in a shoot-out. I have had fights so severe, that I broke the batteries in my flashlight hitting a guy over the head, because he was high on drugs and he was going to kill me. I have seen a lot of dead children. Sometimes, the children were overdosed by their own parents. I have seen many dogs chewing up people, sometimes our own police dogs. Car chases were not fun either.

There were around three times that I had to get people out of burning buildings and apartment buildings; sometimes it was successful, other times they were already dead. I had a guy, one time, fall down right in front of me and couldn't breathe and get air, so I had to give him the first part of CPR, and get his air passage open. Thankfully, he lived. There were multiple occasions when I had to get medical aid to people that were critically injured that were either shot or had trauma from violence. Sometimes, there was trauma from car accidents. If I didn't get them medical attention, they'd die.

Now that I've retired, my life is a whole lot better. I don't even want to go to downtown Indianapolis anymore. When I retired, I had a lot more time to work on the house, which was beneficial. I got to spend more time with my grandkids and I enjoyed the heck out of that. Once Angie, my wife, retired, we got to spend more time together until medical problems started piling up on us. But overall, it is a much better life retired, than working as a police officer. I was just getting too old for it. I was sixty, and you can't wrestle down young people that are high on drugs or anything like that at that age. I just couldn't do it anymore and I realized it. You can either get some office job and sit on your butt, which I couldn't do or retire, and I decided to retire.

Most of the people that thanked me for doing my job, were the people I arrested. They appreciated that I treated them like a human being, and made it as comfortable as possible to go to jail. Now that sounds kind of funny, but it's true. We would let people perform certain functions before they were arrested, and you can use your imagination on what those functions may be and you probably wouldn't be wrong.

Being a young cop these days is tough. I'll be honest with you, I am glad that people have the enthusiasm to do the job, or we would be in trouble, but I feel sorry for them at the same time. The politicians that make the laws, and all the laws in the world won't protect all citizens, but unless we get a lot more jails and keep the assholes off the streets, all the cops in the world aren't going to do any good. It was already a revolving door in Marion County. Many times they would be free on the street after I made an arrest before I even got to go home. So, there is no deterrent for crime and so crime will continue to build up. There are a lot of shootings today, and we had a lot back then too, but the cops could do something about it and it kinda kept a lid on things. They can't keep a lid on things anymore, the politicians who keep making these laws make it impossible to enforce because there are no jails.

www.ingramcontent.com/pod-product-compliance
Ingram Content Group UK Ltd.
Pitfield, Milton Keynes, MK11 3LW, UK
UKHW051133260726
13967UKWH00010B/3018

9 781435 784741